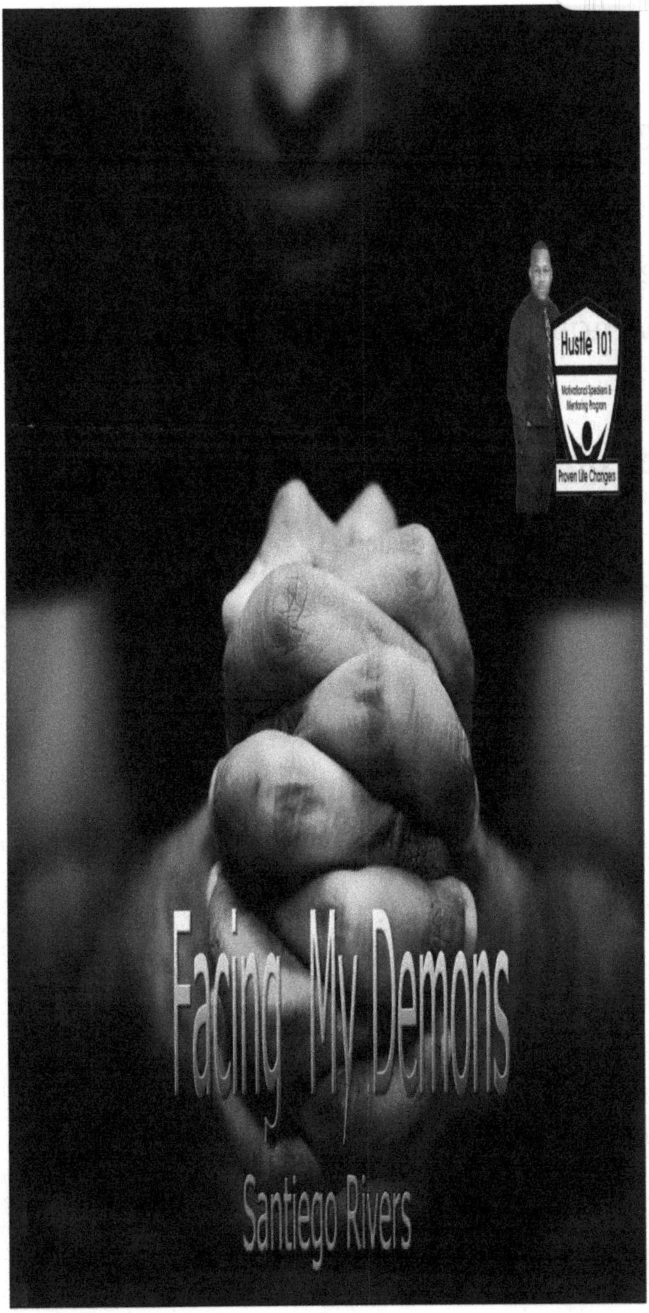
Hustle 101
Motivational Speakers & Mentoring Program
Proven Life Changers
Facing My Demons
Santiego Rivers

Facing My Demons

Copyright © 2021 by Santiego Rivers

All rights reserved. This book may not be reproduced or transmitted in any form without the written permission of the author.

"no copyright infringement is intended."

ISBN 978-1-7376037-4-0

Every day I fight against myself in every way.

Every day, I'm fighting battles in my mind while my smile tries to hide the troubles in my soul that refuse to go away.

Every day, I am prepared to go to war with the demons within me because I know that the God above expects nothing less of me each day.

Every day, I work to claim victory even when victory seems so far away.

I don't know what tomorrow will bring, but today I will face all the troubles that have burdened me in every way, starting today.

Facing My Demons

The strongest people you know face many battles and obstacles that you don't know they are dealing with each day.

Behind their smile hides a pain that has left a stain on their soul over the years.

This book will bring the reader one step closer to understanding the pain behind the smile of our strongest soldiers and the battles they face each day.

This book will say with words all the things that their pride, fear, and pain won't let them share with other people because they feel that they would never understand.

How can someone get others to understand things that they have yet to grasp themselves?

People will better understand you when you are willing to open and give others a chance to know what you feel inside.

Are you willing to let others know?

The bad moments to the good moments and most time even back to the bad moments in your life?

(This makes perfect sense to those people who think like me)

There are no magnificent poetic words that can describe the hurt and pain in my soul, so I will tell you that I am hurting.

Right now, I am in so much mental pain that I wish that it was physical pain because it would make more sense to me.

I need what I am feeling and going through to make sense to me because this pain does not make any sense to my mind, heart, and soul.

My mind, heart, and soul rarely agree on anything, but this uncertainty they do!

What do you do when it feels like your mind is attacking you? The one gift given to you to help make sense of the world around you has become the curse at the center of your demise?

What do you do when you don't know what to do so you don't do anything but sit around and wonder what you would do if you could do anything about your current situation?

(This makes perfect sense to those people who think like me)

My mental demise started a long time ago in my youth, but a recent event brought me back to feeling like a lost and helpless child.

One of my biggest fears was going back to feeling like a lost and helpless child.

(This makes perfect sense to those people who think like me)

Life is filled with many things that will trigger us in different ways. If we are lucky enough to find coping mechanisms to help us deal with the ups and downs that life's rollercoaster puts us on, we may survive the ride without losing our lunch.

I have lost my lunch, my desire, my hope so often that I wouldn't say I like going to amusement parks anymore because they are a negative trigger in my life that I do not need.

(This makes perfect sense to those people who think like me)

Sometimes life, makes us experience things and deal with things that we are not willing or ready to face.

Sometimes life takes people out of your life that you were still trying to get to know. Going through these things makes you feel like a victim again because you have no control over the experience.

You again become that lost and helpless child, and this is a trigger for you.

(This makes perfect sense to those people who think like me)

Can someone or anyone riddle me this for my peace of mind:

When you lose your best friend, your lover, and your wife, why does it change your life?

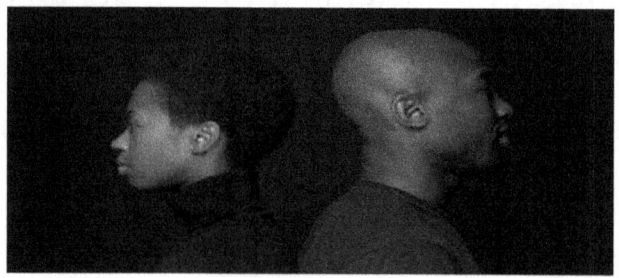

I'm still trying to figure this out for my sanity.

When I first got divorced, I worried about many different things, but none of those worries included worrying about myself.

I worried who would be there to check on my wife when I was no longer there?

Who would make sure that she is eating, getting out of the bed, getting some fresh air each day, or simply being there to let her know that someone cared enough to be present in her darkest moments?

I also worried about what other people thought about our situation. Did they wonder why we couldn't work things out?

Why couldn't we work things out?

I worried about the opinions of the people who supported our union. I even worried about the views of those who did not support our marriage.

I worried a lot. The one thing that I did not take the time to worry about was how I would feel after the divorce became finalized?

It took me a while to realize that the only thing that mattered when it came to our divorce is what God knew about me and my love for my ex-wife. This thought would ultimately give me a reason to smile even though my world was crumbling to pieces.

My peace was in pieces, and I did not know how to begin to put the pieces back together again to restore my serenity.

Finding a reason to smile during adversity is the only thing that will get you one step closer to achieving inner peace.

I desperately need peace in my life!

I held so much inside for years because letting out my anger and emotions scared me to my core.

When I look in the mirror, I don't see the beautiful soul behind my smile. I only know the pain in my heart that my eyes cannot hide.

The only thing that I fear on earth is me!

I wanted to see and feel that joy and happiness that my smile presented to the world that my heart was void of.

I needed to be that beautiful soul that I was created to be; for my sanity, physical and emotional well-being.

It took me some time, but I am coming to realize the following:

You can't pray for victory while operating in defeat.

I have stood; I have sat; I have cried and complained to the God in heaven; why must I experience so much pain in my life even when I am still trying to appreciate the blessing that comes with just being alive?

(This makes perfect sense to those people who think like me)

I needed to change my mindset to change the current situation that I was facing every day because this feeling that I was feeling was not healthy for me.

Those feelings of anger, hopelessness, and despair only put me in a place that did not serve my greater good.

I had to understand that God will never bring me to any place or make me face anything that he felt that I could not survive.

I may not have wanted to be in every place that he allowed me to go, but I needed to understand that he was putting me where I needed to be until I was ready to be where he wanted me to be.

I must admit that I have learned the hard way that:

Challenging roads lead to beautiful destinations!

On my journey, I discovered that my job was to make sure that I did not get stuck in those places that I did not want to be for too long and learn the lessons I needed to know while I was there.

We often revisit old destinations because we failed to learn the needed lessons that we needed to remember when we were there before.

Life is about elevating and changing, so I had to be willing to elevate and change my ways and thoughts to grow in every aspect of my life.

I had to swallow my pride, face my fears, and shed all the tears that I needed to cry to move forward in my life and experience growth.

I should never expect to move forward in my life when I thought the time was right but move forward in my life when God felt that the time was right for me to move forward.

My journey to inner peace has taken me all around the world just to find the courage and the strength to look within to find my happiness.

I hope and pray that:

(This makes perfect sense to those people who think like me)

There's a darkness in me that holds my soul tighter than the grip of a drowning man.

(This makes perfect sense to those people who think like me)

I can't shake it; I can't fake it or even hide from it. It seems that this darkness is always present in my life.

I often wonder why do I continue to live with this gloom in my life?

Unfortunately:

(This makes perfect sense to those people who think like me)

Father,

Forgive me for picking up what I have already laid at your feet

I am so guilty of doing this because the way that my heart feels doesn't always agree with the way my mind works, which often puts a heavy burden on my soul.

(This makes perfect sense to those people who think like me)

Too often, I have started my day off with broken pieces of yesterday trying to solve today's problems, only succeeding in creating new problems in my life.

Too long, I have lived in the prison of my mind, which is far worse than any physical confinement of my body.

The four walls of my home have become the walls of my self-made prison, which imprisons me mentally, physically, and emotionally.

The enemy within my mind is greater than the enemy outside of my home. Over time, I have become my worst enemy.

The once place that was supposed to give me comfort, serenity, and peace only holds me in an area that I no longer want to be.

I have pushed people and loved ones away because I didn't want them to suffer by trying to help me out of a hole that I was unsure if I desired to escape.

I slept my days away because my nightmares begin the moment that I opened my eyes.

(This makes perfect sense to those people who think like me)

I have always been strong in faith, but I admit that the mind, body, and soul can only take so much pain and suffering before reaching its limit.

I understand that adversity is supposed to make us stronger and that the Most High never gives us more than we can bear, but there are times that I do wonder if he had me confused with another soul because mine is barely surviving.

(This makes perfect sense to those people who think like me)

I try to stay around positive people as much as I can, but I admit that my demons and worries keep me to myself a lot because I don't want to bring others down to my current level of despair.

I pray a lot, try to do activities that make me happy, read and watch motivational materials and quotes, but the demons in my mind are always present when I try to be the best version of myself.

It took me some time to admit that my biggest fear was that all the negative voices in my head were right about me.

- **Who am I to be great?**
- **Who could love someone like me?**
- **What makes me worthy?**
- **Why am I even alive?**

Facing my fears meant that I must answer all these tough questions to remove the dark cloud and the negative voices from my head.

Who Am I to be great? I am a child of God, who he created in his image and likeness to be great because he is exceptional himself.

Who could love someone like me? I have first to love myself because self-love is the only love that matters. I must learn to love the not-so-good qualities in me as I love the excellent attributes of myself.

I am working on this daily
(Keep me in your prayers)

What makes me worthy? The fact that God created me and each day my eyes open to a new day to become a better version of myself than I was yesterday. My God does not make mistakes, so I must learn that he did not make a mistake with this broken soul.

The one thing we must be willing to accept is that we will never be fixed or completely whole. So we must find a way to be okay with that. We must make the most of our life each day.

Why am I still alive? I am alive because my God felt that my presence was needed despite my feeling of even being wanted. Therefore, I must come to trust Gods' plan and not give in to my doubts and fears. If I continue to trust him, all of God's plans will be revealed to me in time. I pray that:

(This makes perfect sense to those people who think like me)

I don't have all the answers, but what I do know is this:

There is a light at the end of the tunnel waiting for you. You must be strong and determined enough to finish the journey and trust in your creators' plan for you.

The road ahead will be difficult! But, as I mentioned earlier in the book, difficult roads often lead to beautiful destinations.

Stop making excuses and procrastinating, and take your first step.

Stop searching for the things that you feel that you don't have in your life. Everything that you need in your life is already there to assist you on your journey.

You and God are there, and that is the only thing needed to reach your destination.

Before, during, and after your journey, thank God for seeing greatness within you even when you had your doubts.

During your storm, you have people praying for you and want to support you in your time of need. But are you willing to allow them to do this for you?

Seek counseling! It is okay to seek counseling, and it is greatly needed. Talking with someone does not make you a weak person. On the contrary, it takes real strength to admit that you struggle in certain areas.

We all struggle in some area of our life. However, only strong people will admit that they need help fixing the area they struggle with.

I pray that you realize that you are special and only you can change the current situation in your life.

I hope, and I pray:

(This makes perfect sense to those people who think like me)

This book is dedicated to **Somone Young** and anyone who is facing their most brutal battle alone.

Seek counseling or talk with someone like I am currently doing. Talking with others doesn't hurt. What hurts you the most is when you hold everything in because it will eventually come out.

www.ingramcontent.com/pod-product-compliance
Lightning Source LLC
Chambersburg PA
CBHW071014160426
43193CB00012B/2054